CLUTTER

LIVING LIFE AND LEAVING THE REST

Copyright © 2018 by Stotra Anubhav
All Rights Reserved

DISCLAIMER

This document is geared towards providing exact and reliable information in regards to the topic and issue covered. The publication is sold with the idea that the publisher is not required to render accounting, officially permitted, or otherwise, qualified services. If advice is necessary, legal or professional, a practiced individual in the profession should be ordered.

This is in terms of a Declaration of Principles which was accepted and approved equally by a Committee of the American Bar Association and a Committee of Publishers and Associations.

In no way is it legal to reproduce, duplicate, or transmit any part of this document in either electronic means or in printed format. Recording of this publication is strictly prohibited and any storage of this document is not allowed unless with written permission from the publisher. All rights reserved.

The information provided herein is stated to be truthful and consistent, in that any liability, in terms of inattention or otherwise, by any usage or abuse of any policies, processes, or directions contained within is the solitary and utter responsibility of the recipient reader. Under no circumstances will any legal responsibility or blame be held against the publisher for any reparation, damages, or monetary loss due to the information herein, either directly or indirectly.

Respective authors own all copyrights not held by the publisher.

The information herein is offered for informational purposes solely, and is universal as so. The presentation of the information is without contract or any type of guarantee assurance.

The trademarks that are used are without any consent, and the publication of the trademark is without permission or backing by the trademark owner. All trademarks and brands within this book are for clarifying purposes only and are owned by the owners themselves, not affiliated with this document.

Dedicated to my father

CONTENTS

INTRODUCTION 1

HOW TO APPROACH CLUTTER 3

LOOKING INTO OUR HOMES AND REMOVING CLUTTER FROM THEM 11

CHANGE IN LIVING CONDITIONS & INHERITING THINGS 16

CLUTTER AND EMOTION 20

CONCLUSION 22

INTRODUCTION

Having a very large excess of possessions, and trying to get rid of it can be a very stressful and overwhelming experience. People often associate words like fear, isolation, shame and helplessness to the process of discarding and getting rid of things that they possess and have attached their emotions to. However in a scenario where you have to cut down on your possessions, it is important to be ready emotionally. We fill our houses, cars, phones, hearts and our minds with clutter, and it is important to consistently aim to reduce it.

Clutter is anything that does not add value to your life. Be it broken CDs, used pens, expired medication, negative and inhibiting thoughts, they are all under the category of clutter. However there might be things that you get value from but you cannot keep them without them adversely affecting your way of life. This is also clutter.

Clutter reflects how people spend their income and also how they view possessions. In well to do countries like USA, this problem is even more rampant.

Contemporary US households have more possessions than any other society. There is another problem that must be addressed. That is the problem of hyper consumerism, or buying large quantities of supplies, 'just in case' they might need them. A person does not need 27 blank diaries and 19 rolls of scotch tape at all points in her life!

We address why people often fail to get rid of the excess or to acknowledge that they are over-encumbered with stuff. Often we try to rationalize why we want to keep things. We also come up with excuses as to why we need to keep something. While we do this because we feel that it will be beneficial to us, this often leads us to a lot of problems.

There are three types of clutter: physical, emotional and spiritual. This book can guide you with various methods and procedures for you to work outside of your emotions and to get rid of the baggage that you hold. That said the majority of the book is about getting rid of physical clutter/possessions in our lives.

Chapters 1, 2 and 3 are practical guides on how to remove clutter with exercises present in chapters 1 and 2. Pay close attention to the exercises as they are the heart of this book. Chapter 4 is more of a description of how our mind works in relation to clutter and possessions. While it is recommended that you read through the fourth chapter, it is okay to skip the chapter to get on to decluttering your life, which is the main objective of this book.

Thank you for purchasing this book and make sure to take full advantage of the knowledge inside.

CHAPTER-1

HOW TO APPROACH CLUTTER

One of the biggest problems while decluttering and getting rid of items is to deal with people's emotions. People often attach some memory or emotion to things that they have owned for a certain period of time, so it is difficult for them to personally get rid of them. Their friends find it easy because they have no attachment. So it is a good idea to get a friend or a professional to come to your home and assess the situation objectively.

Along with bringing some company, add a bit of objectivity to yourself as well. Use a rule or an algorithm to which you can adhere. Then you will have a clear idea of which items you need to discard and which ones need to stay. My own algorithm is given at the end of the chapter.

Getting rid of clutter takes time. Anyone offering an instant solution to this problem is probably taking you for a ride. Doing it over a week or even a weekend is possible, but it will be stressful, mentally and physically exhausting, and the result might not be up to your expectations. Create a routine for decluttering by giving an hour of your time every week to decluttering. Be honest to this schedule and consistently put in the one hour, and you will see change.

Some people feel like that they do not have enough time in their lives to deal with clutter. Rearrange your schedule to make time for decluttering. Decluttering is a skill that you can learn and apply throughout your life, so you simply have to stick with it. If it is affecting your life then it surely deserves your time.

Removing clutter can seem like an absolute chore. But it might not be a chore if you succeed in setting up a routine.

There is a difference between clutter and organization.

Organizing is when you arrange your possessions in a systematic manner. Decluttering is simply getting rid of stuff that does not have any value in your life.

Having clutter does not mean that you are messy and being messy doesn't mean that you have clutter. Organizing is temporary and decluttering is rather permanent, since the stuff that you got rid of is gone forever. But even decluttering is temporary when looked at over a long period of time. This is because the things that you own and acquire will eventually become clutter, as your personal likings and priorities will change.

There is a difference between decluttering and minimalism.

Minimalism in a broad way can be described as living with the bare essentials - having as less possessions as possible. If it is not necessary for your life then it cannot be included in a minimalist lifestyle. Many people have a different meaning attached to minimalism but it always has the theme of having only the bare essentials.

Decluttering is actually considered the first step towards minimalism. While decluttering we move away from stuff that we have but don't derive any value from, towards things that are of value to us. Decluttering concerns things that have value in our lives, while minimalism is about need. Clearly decluttering is not minimalism.

EXERCISE 1

THE ALGORTIHM

1. What would you replace if you lost everything? Only add the items that you will buy again if you lost everything. Try and do this without looking at the items in your house. This forms your primary list of things. The other steps below make your secondary list.

2. Does this item do something that no other item does? If the item is unique and adds value to your daily life, only then should you keep the item.

3. Do you have anything else that does this better, or at least does something else as well? Compare those items and only keep the one that adds maximum value to your life in the form of functions or quality to your life. Donate/sell/get rid of everything else.

4. Does the item have sentiment attached to it? Letting go of items around which we have built attachments is a hard thing to do. Alternative is to digitize everything.

5. Purge all items not in your primary or secondary list. It's pretty straightforward. Now that you have personally evaluated every item in your household, and selected which ones you can live without, it is time to discard those items.

6. Do not delay the purging of items. Many people hoard a bunch of stuff because they think it is worth some money and they can make a certain amount of money by selling it. If you think you can sell it, for how much? Suppose selling something will take 'x' amount of time, is it worth it? Or are you just better off discarding the stuff? If it isn't worth the waiting time, then just discard. Otherwise, try to sell on eBay or other websites.

HOW TO IMPLEMENT THE ALGORITHM

Start by making a list. Make two divisions - primary list and secondary list. Jot down all items based on step 1 into primary list.

Now move on and put an item that you would want to keep into the list. There will be parameters to decide whether the item belongs in the secondary list or not.

A list template along with directions is given below.

DIRECTIONS FOR LIST TEMPLATE

1. First list all the things that you will buy again if you lost them at the top of your head. This is your primary list.

2. Now start with the secondary list. Based on the questions in boxes 1-3 , place a check mark if your answer is yes and leave the box unchecked if your answer is no.

3. If box 3 is checked then keep the item.

4. If box 3 is not checked and box 1 is checked, get rid of the item.

5. If box 1 and box 2 are checked but box 3 is not checked, then get rid of the item.

This algorithm will only work if you adhere to it strictly. If this algorithm is a bit harsh you can check the steps in the next chapter.

LISTS FOR EXERCISE 1

Primary List

No.	Item
1	
2	
3	
4	
5	

Secondary list

No.	Item	Is it unique?	Is there something else that can do more or something else?	Does it have sentimental value?
1				
2				
3				
4				
5				

Note: You can change the table size according to the number of items that you want to include in the lists given above

CHAPTER-2

LOOKING INTO OUR HOMES AND REMOVING CLUTTER FROM THEM

In this chapter we provide an alternative to the algorithm mentioned above. We systematically go through various parts of a home and give a detailed list of the stuff that is to be discarded in different spaces. Other important things like paperwork are also discussed. Discussion is limited to the things that you already own. For things that you have inherited, go to Chapter 3.

TAKE OUT THESE ITEMS

1. Old shoes: Shoes often don't age well and you are not doing yourself a favor by wearing them or keeping them in your house. Get rid of them.

2. Clothes you've almost never worn/cannot fit into anymore: Have you kept any clothes that you dislike or don't wear very often? It is probably time to let go of them. If you have clothing you can't fit into anymore, then save yourself some space and do away with them.

3. Books you have never read: If you purchased a book about 12 months ago and still haven't read it, chances are that you might never do so. In this scenario it is better to discard as you can only have a few select items that you can keep.

4. Old toys: Parents often hoard their children's toys. This is because of the sentimental value attached to them by their parents. Though it might be hard to let go of them because of the nostalgia, it is important to do so.

5. Expired products including medication: These items should at no cost be used (especially medication). Systematically group expired items into a trash bag and send them on their way out.

6. Previous year diaries/calendars: If you didn't use it last year, chances are you won't use it ever, especially with the brand new diary or calendar that you have now got.

7. Clear up dry and broken pens: We all have pens that are empty, broken or those that we dislike. We never use them and so one should get rid of them.

8. Clear out junk drawers: Junk drawers full of un-needed items like rubber bands, old batteries, wires and chargers of gadgets that no longer work.

9. Ugly decorations: Decorations that you feel do not look good should be taken out.

10. Do it with the seasons: Seasonally declutter your house, at the change of every season.

11. Buy less stuff: It's simple. Resist the urge to add to your clutter by buying things that you don't need. If it has a function, try and discard something else from your possessions.

KITCHEN

1. Odd spices: Out with all the old funky spices that you kept for cooking one special recipe!

2. Keep the pans that you use: Only 2- 3 pans are used daily, if you make a certain dish which requires a certain utensil or gadget every year (like for July 4th or the Super Bowl) you can keep that utensil. The rest you need to discard.

3. Give every item a home: Have an assigned place for each category of dishes/ingredients/cutlery/gadgets in your kitchen in a planned layout. That way you will have an idea as to where to keep a certain item.

4. Return the items to their place: Once you are done using something return it to its assigned location immediately, so that you are left with one less thing to do in the end.

5. Keep the countertops clean: Always avoid crowding out the countertops as you only have limited space. Return items you won't need any further back to their respective places.

6. Clean right after you finish: Once you are done with cooking make sure that the kitchen is clean so that when you come back next time you won't have to clean it.

7. Don't let your sink fall into chaos: The sink might be an anchor for your kitchen, littering it can lead to litter in the kitchen and vice versa.

PAPERWORK

1. Legal Documents: Any legal documents should be kept.

2. Tax related documents: All documents that could be filed for tax returns should be kept.

3. Evaluate your subscriptions: Take a careful look at your magazine and newspaper subscriptions as well as newsletters that you receive, if you don't read the magazines then it's time to cancel your subscription.

DIGITIZING YOUR MEMORIES

1. Digitize photos and documents: You can scan your old photos and documents to form digital copies. Digital copies can be stored in a small yet powerful hard drive.

2. Digitize movies and music: CDs/DVDs can take up whole shelf loads of space. Try the alternative. And next time you're tempted to buy a physical copy of any of these items opt for the digital one instead and use the physical copies as the last resort. Seriously, music streaming is the future now anyway.

3. Turn books into e-books: Many e-book facilities are out there, like kindle, that let you read anywhere and you are free from having a physical copy with you. Plus once you have bought it you have access to it forever, in case you want to read it again, so you don't have to worry about losing your book.

4. Clear up your email inbox: Unsubscribe to subscriptions and newsletters. I personally feel like it grinds my gears to see hundreds of unanswered mails along with junk mail and newsletters.

EXERCISE 2

In this exercise go through your possessions, apply the rules given above and purge all the things that are advised against keeping. The second part of the exercise is to digitize physical versions of photos, videos, movies and important documents that are to be kept. This will ensure that you retain these items with them occupying any space. If it is costing you money to digitize something (like a book/ movie), it is upon your discretion.

CHAPTER-3

CHANGE IN LIVING CONDITIONS & INHERITING THINGS

This chapter addresses two problems: Moving out of your current house and inheriting possessions from relatives after they pass away.

MOVING OUT

Whether you are moving into a smaller house or you are upsizing into a larger house, it is important to give yourself a fresh start and consider the moving cost for all of the goods that you will transfer. Take this as an opportunity to rid yourself of all the things that you don't want anymore, because it is easy to dispose of things at this time.

The algorithm given in Chapter 1 would be of use here.

1. Begin categorizing and packing a few months before your move. This way the process of moving won't be as tough and exhausting as it would be if you did it over a weekend.

2. Moving costs money, ask yourself if you want an item in your new fresh place and whether you want to pay to get it to your new home. Consider it as an opportunity to start new with new things instead of old ones.

3. First pack the things that come right out of the top of your head and would buy again if you lost them i.e. create your primary list of items. If you think you will have more space in your new home, move on to creating your secondary list.

4. Avoid packing liquids into boxes as they could leak onto other items. In general, you are better off skipping your old grooming products while moving.

5. Keep adding to the secondary list till you have space.

6. There are certain things that you should leave behind such as fittings, carpeting or lighting fixtures or any other elements intrinsic to the house itself.

EXTRA: MOVING INTO A DORM

It can be a daunting task to decide what things to bring when you go to college for the first time. Try the steps below to see if it helps:

1. Due to its limited size, bringing home appliances to your dorm is not the best option, try and use the appliances in the common areas.

2. Try and bring half the clothes you own. This is a matter of personal choice, but people generally wear less than half their clothes on a daily basis.

3. Avoid bringing your whole arsenal of grooming supplies, instead buy over there by assessing how much you can store in your dorm.

4. You will have limited storage space in your dorm. So have a good estimate of how big your room will be, and pack accordingly.

5. Leave behind the physical versions of books, music and photos for digital versions. You can have a lot more for a lot less space with digital media.

6. Don't bring large collections of photos, books, and trophies to your dorm. Chances are you will be cramped for space if you do so.

INHERITING

Passing away of a loved one can be very tough mentally and emotionally. While you deal with the stress, you also end up with things that the person willed to you.

Usually, it is impossible to include everything that they have left you inside your home. Here it is important to only keep things that are meaningful to you and things that remind you of the person. How to deal with the things that you inherit is solely your decision. Here are some pointers:

1. Family photos: You can sift and recycle photos of people or things that you do not care about. Another way is to scan and digitize the photos.

2. Furniture: Furniture takes up a lot of space. So it is advisable to be as conservative about taking these items into your house. Take only what you would like to keep and have space for. Avoid cramming in furniture inside your house. There is no way for you to take in a household load of furniture and move it into your house unless you discard some of your existing furniture.

3. Documents: You have to sort the documents and also separate legal and financial paper from the junk mail and miscellaneous paperwork. Be sure to examine every bit of paperwork as some very important documents could be hidden within them.

4. Heirlooms: Valuable items such as heirlooms and other forms of jewelry are generally kept. Again, it is all up to you. Other objects like cars and such are also upon your discretion.

5. Knick-Knacks: These items would come in the category of miscellaneous. I would advise you to keep things that are the most meaningful to you and also things that remind you of the person who passed away.

6. Collections: Large collections of items like books, plates and trophies should be dealt with keeping in mind whether you actually want those things. If you don't it is advisable to do away with the majority of the collection.

CHAPTER-4

CLUTTER AND EMOTION

Accumulating clutter or 'hoarding' is a mental disorder. Hoarding is also associated with multiple other mental disorders such as depression and anxiety. This hoarding mentality is often seen in people whose parents were hoarders. Hoarding is a subconscious reaction to a past of scarcity. It provides to those people a sense of security against any future scarcity.

The US has a growing business of storage units, a business that did not flourish until recently. This also shows a trend of accumulation among US households.

We are very conflicted when it comes to our possessions. While we may want to keep all of our possesions, we also burden ourselves at the same time by not letting go. Like expressed before, we attach an emotion to certain objects. Some people attach human like qualities to inanimate objects. This way they attach themselves to the object as if it was a person who they know. This makes parting with the object painful. We cling to an experience or a feeling that we felt in the past, by not letting go of certain possessions as well.

Why not let ourselves have new experiences? Why limit ourselves to the happiness we felt only in our past? Form a memory of your precious things, in the form of a photo or a video, and let them go. This way you have that memory of the object without having to deal with the object itself. Let new experiences replace old ones and you will have to deal with significantly less clutter.

Sometimes one's interests change. Like a child's interest might change from having toys to having sports goods. Acknowledge that you no longer have an interest in keeping your 'toy collection'. Perhaps some other person is out there who would gain more joy from having your collection than the joy you have now. Collections symbolize knowledge, identity and value. Letting go symbolizes change in these fields and it is only natural for it to happen.

Another aspect of hoarding is the influence of media on our minds. Often we are seduced by advertisements for attractive products. If we look carefully, most products shown to us always seem to offer a solution to a problem. This tells us something important. We accumulate items looking for a solution.

Clutter can also represent that you are postponing something. We might hold on to an image of ourselves in our clutter. We keep running away or postponing things that we should be doing (like losing weight) by just stashing away an item which reminds us of what we should be doing, and telling ourselves that it is okay to do it later as you would still have that item.

Decluttering brings in a fresh breath and a sense of newness. It symbolizes change. Not only in the amount of possessions that we have but also change in mindset and lifestyle.

CONCLUSION

Thank you again for downloading this book!

I hope this book was able to guide you on how declutter your life using the content in this book as well as the exercises. The next step is to organize your possessions, and seasonally declutter your house. Remember that it is a skill that can help you throughout your life.

Finally, if you enjoyed this book, then I'd like to ask you for a favor, would you be kind enough to **leave a review** for this book? It'd be greatly appreciated!

Thank you and good luck!

www.ingramcontent.com/pod-product-compliance
Lightning Source LLC
Chambersburg PA
CBHW071729020426
42333CB00017B/2452